In Celebration Of.

&

Our Guests & Memories

Our Guests & Memories

Our Guests & Memories

Our Guests & Memories

Our Guests & Memories

Our Guests & Memories

Our Guests & Memories

Our Guests & Memories

Our Guests & Memories

Our Guests & Memories

_____

_____

_____

_____

_____

_____

_____

_____

_____

_____

Our Guests & Memories

Our Guests & Memories

Our Guests & Memories

Our Guests & Memories

Our Guests & Memories

Our Guests & Memories

Our Guests & Memories

Our Guests & Memories

Our Guests & Memories

Our Guests & Memories

Our Guests & Memories

Our Guests & Memories

Our Guests & Memories

Our Guests & Memories

Our Guests & Memories

Our Guests & Memories

Our Guests & Memories

Our Guests & Memories

_____

_____

_____

_____

_____

_____

_____

_____

_____

_____

Our Guests & Memories

Our Guests & Memories

Our Guests & Memories

Our Guests & Memories

Our Guests & Memories

Our Guests & Memories

Our Guests & Memories

Our Guests & Memories

Our Guests & Memories

Our Guests & Memories

Our Guests & Memories

Our Guests & Memories

_____

_____

_____

_____

_____

_____

_____

_____

_____

_____

Our Guests & Memories

Our Guests & Memories

Our Guests & Memories

Our Guests & Memories

Our Guests & Memories

Our Guests & Memories

Our Guests & Memories

Our Guests & Memories

Our Guests & Memories

Our Guests & Memories

Our Guests & Memories

Our Guests & Memories

Our Guests & Memories

Our Guests & Memories

Our Guests & Memories

Our Guests & Memories

Our Guests & Memories

Our Guests & Memories

Our Guests & Memories

Our Guests & Memories

Our Guests & Memories

Our Guests & Memories

Our Guests & Memories

Our Guests & Memories

Our Guests & Memories

Our Guests & Memories

Our Guests & Memories

Our Guests & Memories

Our Guests & Memories

Our Guests & Memories

Our Guests & Memories

Our Guests & Memories

Our Guests & Memories

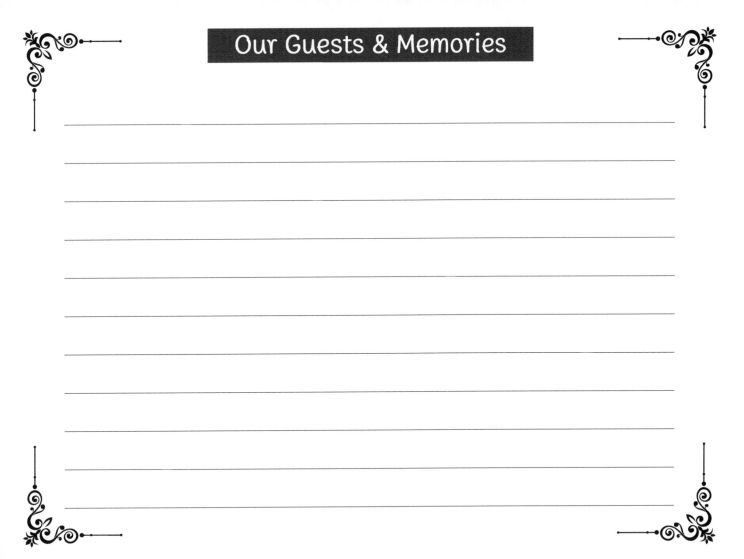

Our Guests & Memories

Our Guests & Memories

Our Guests & Memories

Our Guests & Memories

Our Guests & Memories

Our Guests & Memories

Our Guests & Memories

Our Guests & Memories

Our Guests & Memories

Our Guests & Memories

Our Guests & Memories

Our Guests & Memories

Our Guests & Memories

Our Guests & Memories

Our Guests & Memories

Our Guests & Memories

Our Guests & Memories

_____

_____

_____

_____

_____

_____

_____

_____

_____

_____

Our Guests & Memories

Our Guests & Memories

_____

_____

_____

_____

_____

_____

_____

_____

_____

_____

Our Guests & Memories

Our Guests & Memories

Our Guests & Memories

Our Guests & Memories

Our Guests & Memories

Our Guests & Memories

Our Guests & Memories

Our Guests & Memories

Our Guests & Memories

Our Guests & Memories

Our Guests & Memories

Our Guests & Memories

Our Guests & Memories

Our Guests & Memories

Our Guests & Memories

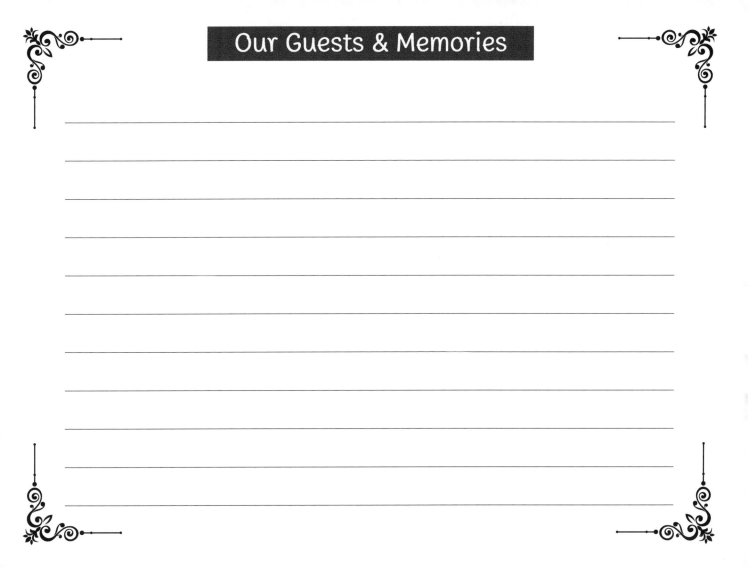

Our Guests & Memories